First Facts®

THE STATUE OF LIBERTY

A 4D BOOK

by Erin Edison

PEBBLE
a capstone imprint

Download the Capstone app!

- Ask an adult to download the Capstone 4D app.
- Scan the cover and stars inside the book for additional content.

When you scan a spread, you'll find fun extra stuff to go with this book! You can also find these things on the web at www.capstone4D.com using the password: liberty.31312

First Facts are published by Pebble
1710 Roe Crest Drive, North Mankato, Minnesota 56003
www.mycapstone.com

Library of Congress Cataloging-in-Publication Data
Library of Congress Cataloging-in-Publication Data is on file with the Library of Congress.
ISBN 978-1-5435-3131-2 (library binding)
ISBN 978-1-5435-3135-0 (paperback)
ISBN 978-1-5435-3139-8 (ebook pdf)

Editorial Credits
Erika L. Shores, editor; Sarah Bennett, designer; Eric Gohl, media researcher;
Tori Abraham, production specialist

Photo Credits
Library of Congress: 13, 14, 15; Newscom: Reuters/Mike Segar, 20; Shutterstock: Chris Parypa Photography, cover, 5, Frontpage, 7, PSboom, 6, Usa-Pyon, 21, Victoria Lipov, 19; Wikimedia: Public Domain, 9, 11, 17

Design Elements: Shutterstock

Printed and bound in the United States of America.
PA017

Table of Contents

A Symbol of Freedom **4**

Designing the Statue **8**

Building the Statue **14**

Lady Liberty Today **18**

Glossary **22**

Read More **23**

Internet Sites **23**

Critical Thinking Questions **24**

Index **24**

A Symbol of Freedom

The Statue of Liberty is a **symbol** of freedom. For many years people came on ships to the United States. They came to start a new life in a new country. They saw "Lady Liberty" when they arrived.

The Statue of Liberty holds a tablet in her left hand. The tablet has July 4, 1776, on it. The American **colonies** declared **independence** from Great Britain on this day. Her right hand holds up a torch.

symbol—an object that reminds people of something else

colony—an area that has been settled by people from another country; a colony is ruled by another country

independence—freedom from the control of other people or things

Liberty Island is home to the statue. The island is in New York Harbor. Ellis Island is nearby and is also part of the Statue of Liberty National Monument. Ellis Island was open from 1892 to 1954. Millions of people came to America for better lives. More than 12 million people entered the country at Ellis Island.

United States of America

Statue of Liberty
New York, New York

Ellis Island

Liberty Island

Designing the Statue

The colonies had won the Revolutionary War in 1783. They became the United States. France had helped the colonies during the war. In 1865 Frenchman Édouard de Laboulaye had an idea. France should give a statue to the United States. It would celebrate America's freedom and the two countries' friendship.

FACT
Édouard de Laboulaye was a leader in France's fight to end slavery.

Édouard de Laboulaye

Scupltor Frédéric-Auguste Bartholdi began planning the Statue of Liberty. Bartholdi had seen the great monuments in Egypt. He wanted his statue to be huge. He designed it to be **hollow** and reach 151 feet (46 meters) tall. He chose copper for the outside. In 1871 Bartholdi visited the United States. He chose a small island in New York Harbor for the statue.

FACT
The Statue of Liberty's copper is about as thick as two pennies stacked together.

hollow—empty on the inside

Frédéric-Auguste Bartholdi

Alexandre-Gustave Eiffel helped design the **frame**. The frame had an iron tower in the middle. Strong bars would join the outside copper to it.

From 1882 to 1884, American architect Richard Morris Hunt planned the Statue of Liberty's **pedestal**. Hunt used concrete for the base. Granite blocks made up the rest of the pedestal.

FACT
Alexandre-Gustave Eiffel also designed the famous Eiffel Tower in Paris.

frame—an arrangement of parts that support and form the basic shape of something

pedestal—a base that something stands on

PEDESTAL FOR BARTHOLDI'S STATUE OF LIBERTY ON BEDLOE'S ISLAND, NEW YORK HARBOR.—DRAWN BY W. P. SNYDER.—[SEE PAGE 359.]

Work began on the statue's pedestal in 1884.

Building the Statue

A group in France raised a lot of money to pay for the statue. But in America, people had a hard time raising money for the pedestal.

Bartholdi began building the statue in Paris in 1875. Many workers helped him. By 1884 it was finished. It was taken apart and packed into 214 crates. It then was shipped to New York.

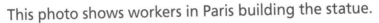
This photo shows workers in Paris building the statue.

After they were finished, the statue's head and shoulders were displayed in Paris.

The pedestal was not done. Publisher Joseph Pulitzer used his newspaper to raise money. It worked. Workers finally put everything together on October 25, 1886.

On October 28, 1886, President Grover Cleveland accepted the Statue of Liberty for the United States. People sailed into the harbor to see it. There was a big parade.

FACT
Pulitzer raised $100,000 in just six months. It was enough money to complete the pedestal.

Boats arrived in New York Harbor to see the new statue.

Lady Liberty Today

The statue has changed over time. "The New Colossus," a poem by Emma Lazarus, was added in 1903. Its famous words welcome people from new lands. In the 1980s, workers fixed the right arm and replaced the torch. They painted the new flame gold.

FACT

Oxygen, or air, has changed Lady Liberty's copper to form a green coating. In 1886 it was more of a brown color, like a U.S. penny.

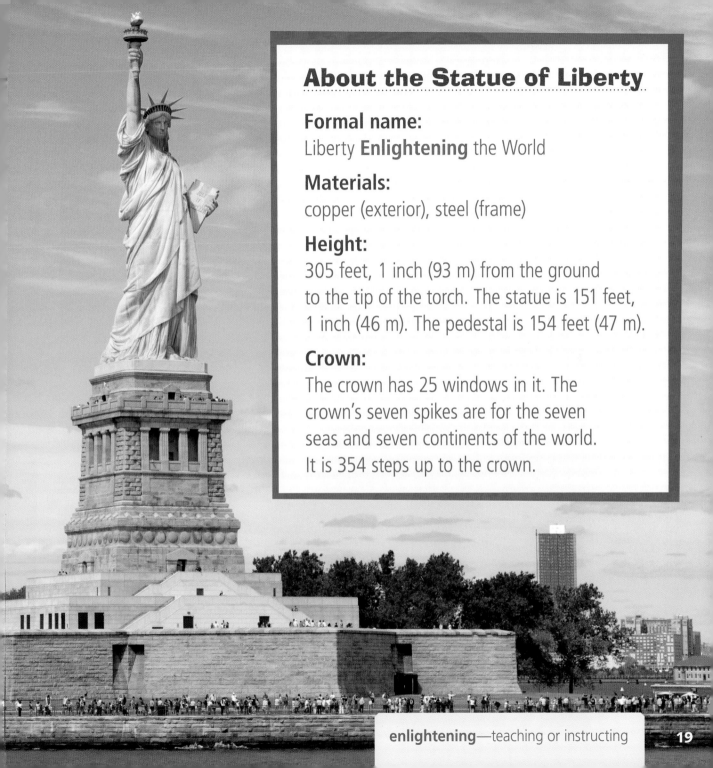

About the Statue of Liberty

Formal name:
Liberty **Enlightening** the World

Materials:
copper (exterior), steel (frame)

Height:
305 feet, 1 inch (93 m) from the ground to the tip of the torch. The statue is 151 feet, 1 inch (46 m). The pedestal is 154 feet (47 m).

Crown:
The crown has 25 windows in it. The crown's seven spikes are for the seven seas and seven continents of the world. It is 354 steps up to the crown.

enlightening—teaching or instructing

Each year 4.5 million people visit the Statue of Liberty National Monument. Visitors take boats across New York Harbor to Liberty Island. Some climb the steps or ride an elevator. They look out from the crown. To people everywhere, Lady Liberty stands for hope and freedom.

Glossary

colony (KAHL-uh-nee)—an area that has been settled by people from another country; a colony is ruled by another country

enlightening (en-LITE-uhn-ing)—teaching or instructing

frame (FRAYM)—an arrangement of parts that support and form the basic shape of something

hollow (HOL-low)—empty on the inside

independence (in-di-PEN-duhnss)—freedom from the control of other people or things

pedestal (PED-uh-stuhl)—a base that something stands on

symbol (SIM-buhl)—an object that reminds people of something else

Read More

Cooper, Sharon Katz. *Gustave Eiffel's Spectacular Idea: The Eiffel Tower.* The Story Behind the Name. North Mankato, Minn.: Capstone Press, 2016.

Ohlin, Nancy. *The Statue of Liberty.* Blast Back! New York: Little Bee Books, 2017.

Internet Sites

Use FactHound to find Internet sites related to this book.

Visit *www.facthound.com*

Just type in 9781543531312 and go.

Super-cool stuff! Check out projects, games and lots more at **www.capstonekids.com**

Critical Thinking Questions

1. Why do you think the Statue of Liberty is a symbol of freedom?

2. Why was New York Harbor a good place for the statue?

3. How did the statue get from France to the United States? Describe the steps.

Index

Bartholdi, Frédéric-Auguste, 10, 14

Cleveland, President Grover, 16
colonies, 4, 8
copper, 10, 18, 19
crown, 19, 20

Eiffel, Alexandre-Gustave, 12
Ellis Island, 6

flame, 18
frame, 12

France, 8, 14

height, 19
Hunt, Richard Morris, 12

Laboulaye, Édouard de, 8
Lazarus, Emma, 18
Liberty Island, 6, 20

New York Harbor, 6, 10, 16, 20

pedestal, 12, 14, 16, 19

poem, 18
Pulitzer, Joseph, 16

Revolutionary War, 8

steps, 19, 20

tablet, 4
torch, 4, 18, 19

visitors, 20